Patrick Henry

VOICE OF THE AMERICAN REVOLUTION

Patrick Henry
VOICE OF THE AMERICAN REVOLUTION

by Louis Sabin
illustrated by Bill Ternay

Troll Associates

Library of Congress Cataloging in Publication Data

Sabin, Louis.
    Patrick Henry, voice of the American Revolution.

    Summary: Focuses on events from Patrick Henry's
youth in the colony of Virginia which proved influential
in his later life.
        1. Henry, Patrick, 1736-1799—Juvenile literature.
2. Virginia—Politics and government—Revolution, 1775-
1783—Juvenile literature. 3. Legislators—United
States—Biography—Juvenile literature.   4. United
States.   Continental Congress—Biography—Juvenile
literature.   5. Virginia—Governors—Biography—Juvenile
literature.   [1. Henry, Patrick, 1736-1799.
2. Legislators.   3. Virginia—Politics and government—
Revolution, 1775-1783]   I. Ternay, Bill, ill.   II. Title.
E302.6.H5S17   973.3 '092 '4 [B] [92]   81-23068
ISBN 0-89375-764-0   AACR2
ISBN 0-89375-765-9 (pbk.)

Patrick Henry

VOICE OF THE AMERICAN REVOLUTION

May 29, 1736 was a golden spring day. The sun warmed the green fields and sent bright arrows of light through tree tops to the forest floor below. The colony of Virginia was a rich land, with plentiful wild game in the woods, clear mountain streams, fertile farmland, and a world of opportunity for its citizens. Anyone born in such a place at that time could look forward to a full and happy future.

This was just the way Sarah and John Henry felt as they looked at their newborn baby. He was a sturdy, round-faced boy with a shock of red hair and sparkling blue eyes. He also had a loud, healthy cry, which filled the room.

"Young Patrick is well named," said Mrs. Henry, laughing.

"Indeed," Mr. Henry agreed. "His voice is the equal of my brother Patrick's. And do you think he will one day be a minister, like his namesake?"

"Heaven knows if he'll be delivering sermons," said Mrs. Henry. "But one thing is certain—people will be sure to hear him!"

Little Patrick quieted down soon enough. He was a bright boy who didn't say very much. But he watched and listened very closely. He would sit quietly, his face very serious, taking in every word spoken by the adults around him.

Patrick heard his father tell about the old days in Scotland, of the poverty he saw when he lived in Aberdeen, and of the dreams that had brought him from the land of his birth to colonial America. In 1707, Scotland had become part of the British empire. But many Scots, like the fiercely proud Henrys, resented their English rulers. They wanted to have their own laws, their own church, their own king.

Patrick listened to his father talk with pride about his family, and how they had fought against the British crown. The Henrys had a strong tradition. They stood up for what they felt was right, no matter how harsh the penalty.

Hanover County, Virginia, was the home of many emigrants from Scotland. From them, Patrick learned many of the customs and ways of his Highland ancestors. He learned to play hard and work hard. He learned never to back off from a fight, never to waste a penny, and always to be fair in his dealings with others.

One of the customs that Patrick enjoyed most was the yearly celebration of Saint Andrew's Day, in honor of the patron saint of Scotland. It was held in the town of Hanover Courthouse every fall. Patrick always looked forward to this fun-filled day.

There were all kinds of contests and prizes. The winning boxer won a hat worth twenty shillings. The winning wrestler got a pair of silver shoe buckles. The finest dancer got a pair of handsome shoes. The prettiest young woman got a pair of expensive silk stockings.

13

A race brought together the twenty fastest horses in the county. There was a drum-playing contest, with the rule that no drummer could beat the drum with his left hand. There was a singing competition. And twenty of the county's best fiddlers entered in a contest, with the top player winning a brand new fiddle. Listening to the fiddlers was Patrick's favorite part of the day. He loved the sound of old Scottish tunes played by the fiddlers. The music pleased him so much that he just had to learn to play the fiddle himself.

Mr. and Mrs. Henry saw that he had a good ear for music, so they gave him a violin. That was all the youngster needed. On his own, he taught himself country fiddling. When he was a teenager he also taught himself to play the flute, the lute, and the harpsichord.

The joy of making music would stay with Patrick Henry all his life. Years later, when he had his own family, they would sit in the parlor and sing hymns every Sunday evening. Patrick's violin accompanied their voices.

The Saint Andrew's Day festivities reached their peak for the youngsters in the late afternoon. As the banquet tables were being set up, sides of beef, wild turkeys, pigs, chickens, and ducks were roasted over roaring fires. The women were busy unpacking hampers filled with pies, puddings, vegetables, fresh-baked breads, and other tasty foods.

17

While all this was going on, there were foot-races for the boys. Year after year, Patrick was among the fastest runners in Hanover County. When he was eight, he had his best running year. He won the Saint Andrew's Day race for boys between ages seven and nine. His prize was a piping hot mince pie, which he proudly shared with his family.

Young Patrick had a good time all year long. On some days he would get together with one or two friends, and they would take their fishing poles to one of the many creeks around Hanover Courthouse. On other days he would go hunting with his father and his older brothers, John and William.

In those days, hunting was not just a sport. The game the Henrys shot might be tomorrow's dinner. Or it might be cured and stored for next winter. Patrick enjoyed hunting all his life. But it was as much for the quiet and beauty of the woods as for the game he brought home.

From childhood on, Patrick loved to wander alone in the woods. He could sit for hours at a time, watching the animals. He was especially interested in birds. He would listen to them chirp and sing, then he would imitate their songs.

Most people were amused by Patrick's clever bird imitations. But some folks in Hanover Courthouse called him "that lazy Henry boy," for spending so much time doing "nothing worthwhile." His parents didn't feel that way. They felt that Patrick was a good boy, and not the least bit lazy when they had something for him to do.

For most children growing up in Virginia in the 1700s, schooling ended when they were about ten or eleven years old. Book learning was not considered necessary to be a farmer, a storekeeper, or just about anything else.

Patrick's education did not end, however, when he stopped going to school. His father became his full-time teacher. And Mr. Henry gave his son a hard course of study for the next five years. John Henry, who had spent four years at Aberdeen University, was a good teacher. And as Samuel Meredith, Patrick's friend and neighbor, wrote later, "Patrick acquired a knowledge of the Latin language and a smattering of the Greek. He became well acquainted with mathematics, of which he was very fond. At the age of fifteen, he was well versed in both ancient and modern history."

Meredith also remembered Patrick as being a quiet, thoughtful boy. Whenever his friends had an argument, Patrick was the one they turned to for a fair, sensible decision. He would listen very carefully to both sides, then take some time to think the matter over. It seemed he took the longest time for thinking when the argument was a really hot one—enough time for tempers to cool on both sides.

Finally, in a soft, reasonable voice, Patrick would give his opinion. He spoke so well that he almost always made both sides happy with his decisions. More than anything else, this skill— to persuade others through words—earned Patrick a good reputation with the young people in Hanover Courthouse.

Another friend remembered the way Patrick looked as a young teenager. "His face was longish and thin. He had a sharp nose, freckles, and eyes as blue as a jay's wing. And you could see Patrick a long way off, with that thatch of hair the color of a ripe pumpkin."

The friend also talked about the way Patrick dressed. "His breeches, coat, and boots were like what we all wore—homespun and plain. But Patrick was different from us in one way. He always tried to keep his shirt and stockings clean. That didn't much matter to the rest of us."

To many of the boys of Hanover Courthouse, Patrick was best known as a practical joker. One time, he caught a young skunk in a trap he had set in the woods. He put the skunk in a straw basket and covered it with a cloth. He brought it to school early one morning and set it on the teacher's desk.

The teacher saw the basket and smiled. He thought it was filled with vegetables, fruit, corn, or animal skins. That was the way parents paid for their children's schooling. The teacher would use what he could and sell the rest.

This time, the teacher was in for a surprise. He lifted the cloth cover and saw two beady, black eyes staring up at him. The teacher was furious. "Who put this beast here?" he roared. "I'll whip the scoundrel!"

The teacher glared at the class and grabbed one of the birch switches he kept near his desk. He whipped it against the desktop in rage. The skunk was terrified by the sharp sound. It jumped out of the basket, lifted its striped tail, and used its famous weapon.

The children flew from the room, the teacher right behind them. School was closed for the rest of that week, and everyone—except the teacher—knew the person to thank for the holiday!

There was no doubt that Patrick had a real gift for talking. His uncle, Isaac Winston, once said, "Patrick, when he speaks, stirs the boys so that I've seen them jump up and crack their heels together, and slam their caps on the ground and stamp them."

Isaac's brother, William Winston, was also a fine talker. His speech-making impressed young Patrick deeply. The boy began by copying his Uncle Billy and soon was the better speaker.

Uncle Billy taught Patrick how to hold the attention of a large group of people. He showed the boy when to speak in quiet tones, when to pause, and when to raise his voice dramatically. And he showed Patrick how to stand and what to do with his hands as he spoke.

Uncle Billy also taught Patrick the ways of the woods. Billy was a true frontiersman. He dressed in buckskin, spent half the year hunting deer, and often lived with the Indians. Sometimes he would take Patrick with him into the backwoods for a week or two. There they camped out, Indian-style, living on berries, nuts, and whatever they could hunt or fish.

Most of all, being out with Uncle Billy gave Patrick a feeling for independence that he could not get anywhere else. The towns and farms of Virginia were very much like the towns and farms of England and Scotland. The habits, clothing, and customs of the people were similar to life in the old country. Here, in the wilderness with his uncle, Patrick discovered a new America. He discovered a new Patrick, as well.

He no longer felt like an English subject living far from the mother country. He felt independent and free. These thoughts and feelings were puzzling to the young Virginian. Sometimes he tried to tell Uncle Billy what was in his mind, but he couldn't find the right words.

"I know what you mean," Uncle Billy told Patrick. "I feel it, too. And I know others who feel the same things. The time is coming—soon—when we'll put these feelings into action. And when that time comes, you'll find the right words to say."

Shortly after he turned fifteen, Patrick got his first real job. He was hired as a clerk in a country store. The Henry family could not afford to send him to college. Even so, Patrick was well educated and ready to begin learning a trade.

The store where Patrick worked sold nearly everything the local people didn't grow or make themselves. Customers could buy corks, saddles, snuff, shoes, silk, eyeglasses, books, salt, tea, mirrors, candle molds, needles and threads, buttons, tools, and other useful items.

Patrick clerked there for a year. In that time, he learned to keep the store clean, to wait on customers, and to do any other task the storekeeper set him to. Then, when he was sixteen, he left the store at his father's suggestion.

"You have done well in your employment," John Henry told his son. "It shows you can succeed at business. And since your brother William is a hard worker, I have in mind that you and he should have your own general store."

"Oh, Father!" Patrick cried. "Do you really think we can do it soon?"

"Yes, I do," Mr. Henry answered. "In fact, I have seen just the place for this store. There is a small house where Newcastle Road meets Old Church Road. Everyone crossing the river must pass that way. There are people on the roads day and night. With good merchandise and hard work, you and William should do quite well for yourselves. I expect you to pay me back in a very short time."

Mr. Henry rented the small house and stocked it with goods to sell. Patrick and William fixed and cleaned the building, inside and out. They built wooden shelves and a counter, then they hand-lettered signs to hang all around the store. At last, the Henry Brothers General Store was open for trade.

As Mr. Henry had predicted, there were plenty of customers. The boys were kept very busy. But they did not make a profit.

In those days, customers paid in money, tobacco, fruits and vegetables they had grown,

game they had shot, and fur pelts. It was common for people to trade for what they needed. Then the storekeeper would sell the goods his customers used as payment. And when they didn't have money or goods to trade, they asked the storekeeper to sell to them on credit. They promised to pay as soon as they could.

Patrick, in charge of the store's finances, gave credit to just about anyone who asked. That brought the Henry brothers a lot of customers. The problem was, Patrick did not demand payment, and he always believed the excuses the non-paying customers gave him.

With very little money coming in, Patrick and William could not buy new merchandise to stock the shelves. They also could not pay back the amount Mr. Henry had loaned them to open the store. After a year of this their father made it clear that he would not lend any more money to such bad managers. So it came as no surprise when the Henry brothers went out of business.

While Patrick was not a success at business, he gained a great deal from the time he spent in the store. Like many frontier general stores, the Henry brothers' place was a popular meeting spot. People would come in to learn the latest gossip, to talk about their crops and the weather, to swap stories and tall tales, and to argue politics.

Patrick was most interested in the political arguments. He was a native-born American, like many of the younger people in the colonies. They weren't like the older folks, who came from Great Britain and had strong ties to the old country. The younger people didn't think about Great Britain as "home." The young and the old often disagreed, and the store saw many a lively debate between them—about freedom, about the right of colonists to make their own laws, and about land.

Anyone who rode west could see endless miles of rich country. It was unsettled and unmapped, but the colonists were not free to live on it. By law, all of this land belonged to the king or to noblemen who lived in England. This angered many of the younger colonists.

Patrick was usually in the middle of the political debates. Because he read so much, he knew many facts. And because he was such a good talker, he was often one of the main speakers. People who defended the king when they came into the store sometimes left with a very different feeling. Patrick's words and the sense he made changed their opinions.

These debates could have made Patrick many enemies. But the tall, lanky teenager was so likable and clever that nobody took offense at his words. More than one listener told him, "Patrick, you ought to be a lawyer. Or maybe you ought to get yourself elected to the House of Burgesses over in Williamsburg."

It was a good prediction of what lay ahead for Patrick Henry. He would become a lawyer, one of the best in the colonies. And one day, in 1765, he would be elected to the House of Burgesses, the colonial legislature of Virginia. There, as the representative from Louisa County, Patrick would stand out as one of the most forceful voices for independence. And, in speaking to this Virginia legislature, he would say the fiery words that would be repeated with admiration throughout the colonies.

Just nine days after Patrick took his seat in the House of Burgesses, he introduced a resolution protesting the Stamp Act. This act placed a high tax on the colonies by the British government. The speech he made, defending his resolution, included these famous words, "Caesar had his Brutus, Charles the First had his Cromwell, and George the Third—"

At this moment, the Speaker of the House cried out, "Treason! Treason!" The Speaker was accusing Patrick of treason for saying that King George should be overthrown as Caesar was overthrown by Brutus and Charles the First by Cromwell.

Those who were present that day remembered how Patrick's blue eyes stared icily at the Speaker. And how he coolly finished his sentence, "—may profit by their example! If this be treason, make the most of it!"

Patrick would make an even more famous— and more important—speech ten years later. By this time the colonies were on the edge of rebellion against England, and King George III

had closed the House of Burgesses. But he couldn't stop the Virginians from meeting and planning their future. The meeting, called the Virginia Convention, was held in Richmond in the spring of 1775. The vote to be taken there would decide if Virginia would support the American Revolution or the king.

The men who spoke against revolution pointed out how war would hurt the colonists. They spoke of the thousands who would die on both sides, saying that American guns would be firing at men who were brothers and cousins. And so, even at the price of freedom, they called for peace.

When it seemed that these Loyalists might win the vote, Patrick Henry leaped to his feet. The hall fell silent. Nobody on this morning of March 23, 1775, wanted to miss a word uttered by this spellbinding speaker.

Patrick spoke of Virginia's noble history, of the patience the colonists had shown each time the king put a heavier burden on them. He spoke of the efforts made by the House of Burgesses, and how the king had scorned them. Then, with these ringing words, he closed his speech, "Gentlemen may cry peace, peace—but there is no peace. The war is actually begun! The next gale that sweeps the north will bring to our ears the clash of resounding arms. Our brethren are already in the field! Why stand we here idle? What is it the gentlemen wish? What would they have?

"Is life so dear, or peace so sweet, as to be purchased at the price of chains and slavery? Forbid it, almighty God! I know not what course others may take; but as for me—give me liberty or give me death!"

47

These stirring words led to an overwhelming vote for revolution. And they were echoed again and again throughout the colonies as other Americans joined in the fight for liberty.

Patrick, who also served five terms as governor of Virginia, continued to be a leading force in the war for American independence. And when he died, on June 6, 1799, Patrick Henry was honored as the most unforgettable voice of the American Revolution.